Kolin was born in North West England and studied at Cansfield High School, Wigan Technical College, Winstanley College and South Trafford College. He has worked as a T.V. background artist and a corporate DJ, as well as a civil servant.

He lived in Athens for two years, working as a singer and semi-professional dancer. He has spent the last five years writing and addressing personal health issues.

The author auditioned for The London Contemporary and The Ballet Rambert. He is a qualified holistic therapist, an advocate of environmental issues, plays the trumpet (strictly for own pleasure), and enjoys 'funky' house parties and quiet nights at home listening to jazz. He finally 'came out' when he was twenty-one.

Dedication

Doreen (Mother)
Peter (Brother)
George (Father)

"Live chasing your potential as it burns more calories and is good for the waistline."

KRH

Kolin Richmond-Hughes

POEMS FROM A MELANCHOLIC PANDA

AUSTIN MACAULEY PUBLISHERS™

LONDON • CAMBRIDGE • NEW YORK • SHARJAH

A CIP catalogue record for this title is available from the British Library.

ISBN 9781528949972 (Paperback)
ISBN 9781528949989 (Hardback)
ISBN 9781528972499 (ePub e-book)

www.austinmacauley.com

First Published (2019)
Austin Macauley Publishers Ltd
25 Canada Square
Canary Wharf
London
E14 5LQ

Acknowledgements

Kate Bush and David Sylvian for the musical inspiration. Auntie Lilly for the prayers. Irene Evens for the support. Melanie, Debbie, Mel, Dave, Jamie and Julie for the laughter. Stephen Clayton for the coffee. Jason Wong for getting me back on the road. The Worboys for the permission. "Starbloomers" for the technical help. Darren, Marcel and Jonty for the fun and Flee, my sadly missed cat.
Ron in America, Jacquie in Canada, Alexia Vassiliou in Greece...and all my family, the Richmonds, Rippons, Partridges and friends...thank you so much.

Table of Contents

Foreword

When asked once how do I best describe my poetry, I had to pause for a moment and replied, "naive melancholy… with just a hint of optimism." Or possibly, "like a shard of light you might see shining through a dark cloud"… Or maybe, "finding your favourite choccy biscuits have been reduced in price just as you start your diet".

Poetry can be found in everything; always have a pencil and paper with you at all times; "it is a fleeting narrative of a fleeting moment and a poet is but a songwriter who can't afford the musicians."

Poetry to me is a literary validation of a moment… I hope you enjoy my shared moments.

KRH

The River Folk

In the cold dead of night...
And the fishes' eyes closed tight.
The shimmer from the platinum moon...
Indicate the river folk will be here soon.
For in the dead of night...
...and the fishes have little to bite.
Nothing is quite as it seems
The 'voices' from the rivers and streams.
The Geese and the Mallards are in the know,
As they transport the river folk to and fro.
Dancing and skipping, singing silent songs...
Only the cry of the vixen indicates something is wrong!
For these are the river folk,
Who deliver your dreams?
In the inky black night
From the rivers and streams.

Love To The Sea

I send my love to the sea
From whence I last saw thee
I made a deposit in Dogger Bank
To the very place my lover sank

Oh Grim Reaper Grim Reaper for I am lost
Landlocked in the mist, sea, fog and frost
The soul of my lover is now Neptune's host
I am but a shadow… a soulless ghost

Landlocked I roam the hills and the vales.
My lover lost in the haze and prevailing gales.
A watery grave is the ocean's gain…
It will never relinquish my aching pain!

Oh fishes of the night please protect his soul.
Deliver him unto me in dreams as I get old.
He will swim with the dolphins happy and free,
My heart is now broken and he had the key.

Girl In A Room

Thirteen pages on the floor
One open window but no door
The girl looks up, open armed,
All is quiet nothing is alarmed.

Empty pages tell no story,
No poems of love nor glory.
The silent girl back to glass,
Time will inevitably pass.

Sun strains through panes of six,
The shadow on the floor a crucifix.
No furniture, no pictures, just a wall…
Thirteen pages and silent girl that's all.

Maybe someone, somewhere knows she's there.
Her complexion pale, with scraped back hair,
Like a miniature statue she stands alone,
Black dress, no shoes, just skin and bone.

If she had a pen to use, to write…
Would she tell of paranoia and fright?
Thirteen pages remain on the floor.
No one will knock as there is no door.

Time will pass, night into day…
Girl in a room will always stay.
Suspended in time as it's always been
One window, one girl… and blank thirteen!

Good Morning?

Wood pigeons coo in the trees
Morning caressed from a summer breeze
The day starts optimistic and bright.
Waking from the dead of night.

Breakfast is the morning dew…
As folk wake with much to do.
Alarm clocks and radios do their thing.
The morning chorus, did once sing.

Clouds, float apart… way up high.
As if stage curtains to a theatrical sky.
A languid stretch from the cat.
Sleepy heads now start to chat.

Teeth are cleaned, showers run.
Through the curtains shines the sun.
The Postman deposits on the mat,
Startling the half-awake pet cat!

Clothes are chosen in a random fashion,
Neither with enthusiasm nor with passion.
One occasion wearing two left shoes,
At the time is did frustrate and amuse.

Breakfast an ordeal we routinely endure,
Coffee, tea, milk, fresh orange then pour.
Garbled niceties are exchanged with haste.
Difficult with toast… or whatever in your face!

"Have a nice day," the couple kiss and say.
School uniformed children, go on their way.
The cat goes fourth into the great outdoors,
Watching the birds with retracted paws.

A good morning like so many others…
Sons and daughters, fathers and mothers.
How I imagine a morning like that…
As I face another day, sat alone in my flat!

Dear Me...

I thought I would write to me to say,
I hope you are alright and okay.
I am sorry I haven't... "for so long."
Hope all is fine and nothing wrong.

It has been some time since we met!
Can you remember?... as I forget...?
I recall you wore blue and scarf of green
'Mocottan' shoes and a stone wash jean.

Conversation meandered from this to that,
By the way, how is your cute precious cat?
Oh how you made me laugh until I cried...
Those funny little anecdotes; I nearly died!

Hope I find you in the greatest of health...
Wishing all the very best in luck and wealth.
We mustn't leave it so long, do keep in touch,
Maybe a meal some time, we will go Dutch!

Well I must not keep you a minute longer...
Seriously you look well and so much younger.
It's all ways a pleasure and it is never a pain,
"Dear Me, can't wait to talk to myself again!!"

Those Voices

We make choices from those little voices…
The consequences of which we learn to abide.
Those little voices that influence our choices
Sadly we learn were clueless and they lied.

Those little voices can take on many visors
Whispering to you at all times of the day.
Persistent little voices full of big surprises
They nig and nag and seem to get in the way.

Assiduous little voices mulling around in your head
Not pausing for breath as they draw on your own…
Most resolute once you retire to your solitary bed…
…their whispering narrative is chilling to the bone!

My conscious, a spirit a cacophony of sound
An inaudible muttering in mute tones they persist
A collection of voices grinding me to the ground
A haunting mist… I need those voices to desist!

Trying to convince me I would be better off dead
I meditate and mediate to silence their behest.
Helpless to those little voices taking over my head
Please leave me alone and give my soul some rest!

On Putney Bridge

In the dark and oh so inky black of night.
Under the covers and eyes closed so tight.
Morpheus and Sandman come to your slumber
To feed your dreams… with all and asunder.

Word has it the ravens flew from the tower.
Aerial broadcasts on each and every hour.
That 'this woman's work' has come to rest,
She joins 'the big sky' she was truly blessed.

A saxophonist laments our heavy loss,
'Under the ice' near the big wooden cross.
'Kashka from Baghdad' hangs his head and cries,
Delius 'symphony in blue' plays to her demise.

She has 'run up that hill, to be 'king of the mountain'
Her voice we will hear, but alas not seen again.
Our 'lion heart' has roared; one last time…
A voice, a beauty that was so unique and sublime.

England will listen and dance while you are away…
Until each and every one of us will join you one day.
We'll come 'cloud busting' to your 'wuthering heights,'
Amongst the stars and those glittering lights.

I recall my time on Putney Bridge, 'tickets in hand'.
With Lewin and Duncombe to hear, the K.T. Band.
The 'fish people' sang from the ninth wave…
A memory I shall carry to my inevitable grave.

"Oh, but cease my haunting melancholic head,
That I dream of the living as if they're dead."

(Dedicated to Claire and Simon)

Civil Servant Soldiers

Nothing worse than a soldier in a suit!
Wearing brogues and not a military boot.
Manipulating the lives of many others…
Yet bring back the bodies of sons of mothers!

The public relations office works with zest…
To pacify the press… 'they're doing their best'.
With innocuous phrases like 'friendly fire'.
The true concept is simply just too dire!

'Blair' spun his speech of tarnished gold…
…and so the war of words were sold.
To an eager public and media ready for fight,
Yet no weapons of mass destruction in sight!

In fact, the only destruction anyone could see,
Was invariably from the likes of you and me.
Onward 'Christian Soldiers' marching as before…
Muslims shell shocked as they pray from the floor.

The kosher media relish the sights and sounds
Vindicated somewhat from those Nazi clowns
So begs the question what did we achieve?
As the planet struggles yet again to breathe.

'Whitehall' and the 'White House', those suits in a seat!
Will check their diaries for another military repeat.
Yet seldom will they go to an actual War…
Far too busy on the golf course… for this 'chore'.

No more wars just military campaigns,
It is the same thing with trendy names.
If God forbid we have a period of peace,
These 'civil servant' soldiers may just decease!

Cancelled Stamp

Cloche hats and flappers dresses.
Everybody wants to look impressive.
Art Deco is simply everywhere…
Cabbage filled wallets, loads to spare.

Giles and Sebastian are ladies men.
Sipping giggle water, alone in the den.
Noel plays something, quite divine,
Ladies powder noses, it is quite a crime!

Peace time blows in on a summer breeze,
Lanterns swing gaily in the trees.
A 'cancelled stamp' didn't get her chance
To drink champagne and to dance.

Not even a 'corn shredder' took the time,
To whisper sweet nothings that did not rhyme.
Twenty years to wait for another 'great war,'
The death toll will sadly clear the floor.

Airmen and Sailors dance to another tune.
She need not worry, her time will be soon
Overlooked by the 'bright young things.'
Mummy's little solders, comfort she brings.

Metal hats and bombed addresses.
Everyone under immense stresses.
Dead bodies and the injured everywhere,
A time of unrest and great despair!

Giles and Sebastian wear feathers of white.
Dance in the dark shadows, of the night.
Coward plays a much different tune,
Of love and hope…may it come soon.

Peace time once blew in on a summer breeze.
The horrors of war whispered threw the trees.
'The cancelled stamp' had her time to shine,
Reassuring the boys they will be fine.

Life is a dance floor for all to share
Some dance alone, couples waltz as a pair
Wait for the music that suits you the best
As the Unknown Soldier is laid to rest.

Our memory forgets the human…inhumanity.
As Hollywood romances the utter insanity!

Poppy Day

So go wear your Poppy with pride
And remember those who died
Pin red paper and plastic of green
For young men that should have been

Sunday in November the time of choice
Where millions of men lost their voice
Marching sombrely with grave concern
Paying homage to those who did not return.

One minute silence around the Christian world
The National flags half-mast and unfurled.
Monarchs and Presidents the Public and Press
Dressed in their finest to express and impress.

To remind us of the sacrifice made for peace
But sadly wars never seem to ever cease.
Cynics may scoff and criticise this parade
As nothing more than a military charade.

Conscientious objectors defiantly said no
The conformists obeyed orders to simply go.
A man with a rifle went off to fight the Hun.
'White feather boys' shot by an English gun.

Peace is what is strived for but never maintained
Soldiers' uniforms are meddled and bloodstained
Graveyards get bigger with each military campaign
War is such a sad waste of life and utterly insane!

So wear your Poppy with pride
Remember the politicians that lied
Monuments adored with plastic and red
To honour those that are sadly dead!

Ergophobia

The relentless collection of twelve marks the hour,
Where the bells do toll, the time to go shower,
Some chirpy music will invade my dreams…
And the news will tell me all is not as it seems.

Gravity is of a 'magnetic mattress' force, of course,
The warm heavenly duvet forces me to pause.
My pillows caress my head and keep me sane,
I hear the morning rainfall upon the windowpane.

The big wide world is no place for the likes of me,
The tedium of 'nine to five'… the point, I cannot see.
A familiar routine prior to all that I must endure,
I just do not think I can cope, of which I am sure.

Feet on the ground, up for a stretch, yawn then go.
Brush teeth, urinate just go with the preverbal flow.
Make haste to the cold stark kitchen to make some magic
Burnt toast, weak tea, it is all rather tragic!

I fall into the wardrobe and wear whatever fits,
Thirty minutes out of bed, I am at the end of my wits!
I open the front door where I simply froze…
As the torrential rain adds to my morning woes!

My corporate routine unfolds before my very eyes,
A flock of 'Helvetica' words fill my mind, mostly 'whys?'
…that I put myself through this tortuous charade,
I contemplated my day ahead and became quite afraid.

Ergophobia a morbid fear of returning to work.
Nothing very exciting being a boring office clerk.
A smart computer being much smarter than me!
Filing endless bits of paper and making lots of tea.

My female co-workers chatting about this and that,
Flicking through periodicals and bitching who's fat.
Blokes re-living football matches and birds they've laid
All the sexes complaining about the money they are paid.

The monotony of it all flashes before my eyes.
The rain clouds fill the vast equally dull skies
I cry out "there has to be more to life than this…"
Or is God having a heavenly laugh and taking the piss!

The lovely people at the DWP will understand, 'I'm sure'
That I walked out of my job because it was an utter bore.
I slammed the door shut… turned on my heels back to bed.
I'd rather be warm and horizontal fast asleep instead!

I no longer hear the rain on the window anymore.
In my open sleeping palm, is my purring cat's paw.
My dreams may not pay well but are an endless delight
My favourite phrase has got to be, "thank you and good night!"

Some People

I don't care for people they fill my head.
I wish they would be quiet and stay in bed.
I do not care for the things that they say…
Oh how I wish they would all just go away!

The 'nine to fivers' and 'stay at home mums,'
Screaming babies and toddlers sucking thumbs.
The 'let's do lunch' and the tedious 'tasters of wine,'
Humdrum lives that are just a waste of time.

My preference is to walk the streets alone…
Seeing no one on their bike or anti-social phone.
People pollutants like pigeons…please fly away.
Cease the prosaic conversations day after day.

Eat, urinate, defecate… watch TV then repeat…
Walking around aimlessly on those stinking feet.
Students fill their heads with pointless knowledge
To finish up unemployed… at the 'DWP College.'

The CVQ credit card consumer, pay their bill,
For their fashionable purchases, to become landfill.
From warehouse, to wardrobe, a recycle of waste.
Shoppers and purveyors of utter bad taste.

Obese, plastic people contaminating, GDP.
I simply do not care, I just wish to be free…
…from those who poach and hunt for fun,
These vile little people, who feel bigger with a gun!

Conversation is exaggerated 'sound bites' and cliché,
But no one is really listening to what each other say.
The vocabulary and content is facile and dull.
The jaw open and closes from their empty skull!

Fornicators are the worst…of this lot…
Breeding like rabbits… from coffin to cot.
The drunk and disorderly do a lot of this sort of thing,
Polluting the planet with their banal "off-spring"

I prefer spaces that are void of their faces
Big, vast, open… people-less, silent places.
The world doesn't need love, just less of you,
…and all the tedious narcissistic things you do!

People are at best, asleep in a graveyard.
No one marking your birthday… with a card.
Your name is resigned, to a piece of stone.
Leaving me in silence, to roam the world alone.

Spiritual Nebula

Without warning the crippling came,
My identity lost I do not recall my name.
All around that is familiar, I no longer know
My voice is silent like screaming in snow.

The energy abandons me... lifeless I feel.
Nothing is the same, nothing seems real.
Head full of voices... needing to be heard.
I wish they would sing silently, as a mute bird.

My body is crushed by the thoughts in my head.
I am a shadow of myself, I am the living dead.
I have no future... the concept scares me to death.
The past is ever present as I lose my breath.

Tears come forth to caress my sad face.
I need to go... and get out of this dark place!
The light forward is not so very clear to me,
Someone has locked life's door and I've lost the key.

Oh, dull the pain that has become my existence
Legs no longer support me I'm spiritually listless.
Gravity pulls my arms down to my side...
I do not know how much more of this I can abide.

Food has no taste and drink quenches no thirst.
My life it feels like it is heading into reverse.
Pleasure is such an alien conception to me.
I am encased in this black mist, I no longer see.

Dark clouds float in a platinum cold sky.
The kind of sky that birds do not fly...
The icy wind that blows... is an ill wind of snow.
It embraces my frail body and brings such sorrow.

Azrael will avoid my mood of darkness
To leave me is but an act of kindness
My demons are my own worst enemy
The depths of hell are no match for me

When the dark cloud descends and encases my head
All is void and pitch of night, my spirit broken… now fled!

Catafalque

Recliner, decliner death repose.
No one notice, one does suppose.
Oil lamp stand, a solitary affaire…
No light, no shadow, no one to care.

The atmosphere, is of mute brown.
A general foreboding of feeling down.
Neglected footstool covered in soot.
Awaits the presence of a foot.

Recliner, decliner death repose.
Where life, has simply froze.
A pale white morose cotton, drape.
Superficial existentialism, escape.

Chaise lounge in shadows bleak.
A place no one comes to seek.
Catafalque reclines and reminds,
Of a life now passed, of happier times!

Lilies lament in an empty jar
Mourners failed to come from afar
A candle flame offers no light
A beating heart, is still as night.

Oppression depression corpse recline.
Hearts now broken… once entwined.
All that was life, comes to this…
A coffin box top… goodnight kiss.

The Incident In The Graveyard

It was a dark and dreary windy night.
The type of night one just might,
Decide all is naught and in vain...
The troubles of life and nagging pain.

An owl hooted to indicate it was there
A nimble fox tiptoed without a care.
A hedgehog settled down for a long night
The church cat illuminated by the moon light.

The wind it spun an icy spell for all
Autumn was coming the leaves did fall
Marble and granite head stones stood alone
All was still... apart from a woeful moan.

A pitiful shape of a man in much despair
Sat hunched clutching rope but no chair
Head in hands he openly sobbed
Life had not been good, he'd been robbed.

No mirth or merriment had been his way
A melancholic woe had a hold of him this day.
The rope was of a fashion to end it all,
Taking some consideration for he was tall.

Without warning he glanced at an old yew tree
He thrust the rope toward the branch, for he...
Spontaneously without care or compassion for himself...
He embarked on his final act without wealth or health.

It was time to say farewell to a cruel empty life.
The note would explain all... to his kids and wife.
Placing his head into the carefully prepared noose,
He stood on a gravestone corner that was loose.

The tears streamed down from his ashen face,
He realised this would be his final resting place.
Stepping from the edge of the moss ridden tomb...
He braced himself for the rope, the snap, the gloom.

Alas our poor soul was blessed with bad luck.
He miscalculated the rope and got rather stuck.
So instead of hanging... he simply just dangled
And was by way far... from the intended strangled!

The night was long but morning inevitably rose,
And the groundsman found him on his tippy toes
With his scythe he cut the man down to the ground
But realised after some prodding there was no sound.

Instead of a quick snap of the neck and all be done,
His demise would have been quicker with a Farmer's gun!
The poor chap had simply throttled himself for some time
It was the length of the rope that had foiled his crime.

The groundsman asked 'had he been hanging around for long?'
"Young man you got your measurements completely wrong"
The sad young man would be distraught by the error he'd made
So the groundsman finished him off with the 'grim reaper's' spade.

So ashes to ashes and dust to dust...
Suicide is possible but maths is a must!

The Nocturnes

I will take you places you never knew
The kind of places that are rather blue.
To show you things that may just surprise
Make you blush and hide your innocent eyes.

Hold out your arm take my hand, trust in me,
To show you things you don't want to see.
Your life has become tedious and routine,
Time for a change and something more obscene

Images and visions that will blow your mind,
As these creatures are not of your usual kind.
Fun time, at night-time, where the nocturnes go.
To a shadowy world lit by a garish neon glow.

Transgenders morphing caterpillars to butterfly
Gay mixed race and black urbanists looking fly
The Long Yang Club Orientals looking West
As Lesbians and Gay Boys all looking their best.

The b.p.m. music pounds with a hypnotic beat
In time, once it kicks in, you will feel the heat.
That restrictive 'hetero' world for now is gone
For you and the nocturnes are now as one.

Sackville Park

Alan Turin sits motionless down in the park...
In a heterosexual world; he left his apple mark.
Edna's cottage for those who would pee...
The only place to express their homosexuality.
The park is small but nicely green.
For gay men and women and fabulous drag queen!
A place to reflect on those that have gone.
The Mardi Gras candlelight vigil, for those who have shone.
Roxy Hart and Ms Galore order more champagne...
Lee Star and Felicia... do not complain,
Gone are the clones, dressed in leather and rubber
... and those pretty boys, the proverbial night clubber.
Zoe 'duffle coat' sits and recalls, Graham and Elaine
Talking to himself... that nothing will be the same.
Damian and Nigel "jump to the left", 'in Essential'
Disco pharmacists "nice one mate let's go mental"
Thorini and Ms Reeny, Geordie...Taylor Brook
Those beautiful sequinned night owls, come take a look.
Winne 'Le Freak' serves up "camp cuisine."
Miss D'Bray, Legs Up Lucy; sing at the karaoke machine.
Alison Jones performs with her dance troop
Entrepreneur Tiger; choreographs the 'mint group'
Tea with Tony, Campari and the smiling Desire.
"Has anyone seen, 'Just Uz"...everyone would enquire?!
Solitaire, Foo Foo, Nanna and Terry Night...
...those fabulous personalities shone so bright.
We thank you Manchester for our Sackville Park...
...as being 'gay' can sometimes be very dark!
Dancing in the shadows are Leroy, Dennis and Pernell,
Urban brothers and sisters, enduring prejudicial hell.
Don't let developers and architects take your Village...
You fought 'Clause 28' and homophobia to keep your image
A safe space to express yourselves ideally.
A place to love, to laugh and to party freely.
So... mirror ball, mirror ball do shine your light...
Bring us some hope and light to our fight.
The Transvestite and Transgender... memorial tree
Is all that we have, to remember... of us, you and me...

My Youth

My heart is with them but my dancing shoes are gone.
The evening sky is full of light but my sparkle has shone.
The energy of youth I sense but time holds me in check.
The body is willing to join the scene but my face is a wreck.

The songs I no longer recognise, it all sounds quite a din.
I just about take part, I no longer have the energy to win.
The fashion is just so fabulous, on me it's a dreadful fright!
I long to be with the 'in crowd'…alas I'm not quite right!

I swing my hips to the rhythm in an attempt to impress,
Those around me looked disturbed and rather distressed.
I soldier on and thrust my arms aloft, to the iconic mirror ball.
Sadly, the rhythm escapes me and to the floor I start to fall.

I was out like a light I was gone for just a moment or two
I scrambled to my feet like an upturned tortoise without a clue.
Humiliation my partner in this 'dance faux pas' it would seem.
I have never been a part of the scenery, life can be so very mean!

So at my table of life, I simply look on alone and forlorn…
At the beautiful people being beautiful, since they were born!
I sometimes yearn to be young and be fashionable once again,
As the call of my youth cries out to me and causes me great pain.

So dance oh youth and enjoy the music, the style while it lasts,
Without warning the fashion will change and a shadow will be cast.
No one will remember the steps of a dance that was once all the rave,
As you slow dance and reminisce your way to that inevitable grave.

Dancing Boy

Oh he was beautiful, the boy in a vest,
Strutting his stuff in front of the rest
His bubble butt, his perky chest
Without a doubt he was the best!

Latissimus dorsi, bicep and traps
Smooth toned skin no need for tats
Off comes the vest his jeans undone
The crack of his arse, you could see his bum.

The dance floor was his and his alone,
Oh how we wanted our name… on his phone.
He smiled, he winked, hips swung side to side.
The 'worthless' just looked on and sighed.

The funky house and the vibrating beat
The testosterone and erections added to the heat.
The bubble butt gym bunny for all to see
Oh how I wished he would leave with me.

Then without warning, it all went wrong
As he seemed to dance to another song.
The funky beat continued in the same way,
But for some reason he did the 'Y.M.C.A'

He minced about in such away,
He looked like a naff, being gay.
His wrist went limp, like a flaccid cock
He became a muscle boy, in a charity frock.

The poppers, the lager, ket, and coke,
He'd crossed that line, it was no joke!
He "oohed and aahed" and waved at who?
No one could help him, as he started to moo!

'Oh bless her', "Oh dear, that's not pretty,"
Came the 'queens' chorus, "oh what a pity."
From 'Tom of Finland' a muscle hunk,
To 'Wendy of Wigan' a wobbly drunk!

"What Happened To Panda"

I used to perform… I used to dance,
I would play good music, given half the chance!
All of which… was done in my former days,
Background artist, to John Arden plays.

Esther… crowned me, 'the national robotic'
To German music, I was quite hypnotic.
To a Canadian lesbian… I would "port de bras"
My singing of "cat people" took me quite far.

Athens became my second home
Whereas now…I performed alone.
My dancing days have now gone away…
… as all of the above, just did not pay.

Deejaying for drunks just lost its appeal,
Playing music of the dead became surreal.
I hung up my dance shoes and silent headphones
… my spirit became weary, I had tired bones.

A 'black and white bear', of the jazz variety…
My equity card gave me professional notoriety.
A proper job, 'civil servant' signing people on.
Eight years, a carjacking, everything just gone!

On the streets, homeless in two thousand and eight,
It was not a good year, it was far from great!
Psychiatrist enquired about suicide, in our weekly chat,
I simply replied "who would look after my cat!?"

Twelve years later, here we are…
A new apartment, and racing green car.
My friends lament, on what I used to be
But sadly those days are no longer me.

Like a solitary tree, in a field I stand alone,
Braving all weathers, past talents have flown.
I have reached a point in my life, of reflection…
… and all past lovers, a collection of rejection.

Friends smile back from an old photograph.
In times now gone where we would laugh.
Many are married, too busy or sadly dead,
Life can be such a bitch, as it is often said...

To conclude, my mantra seems to be, "I used too"
That part of my life delivers me to pastures new.
A life of empty, months, weeks and days...
The past, a vague memory and distant haze.

I used to live a life of optimism and hope...
Now I view the future through my horoscope!

(Dedicated to Panda Jazz my former alter ego)

After the Mardi Gras

Now the rainbow flags have flown and gone.
The clouds regroup as the sunshine shone.
Cobbled streets empty from all the litter…
Optimism relents and replaced with 'bitter'.

The bars now empty the lights are still…
Managers start to count the cash in the till.
Door staff and bar boys go home to rest…
Take off their ties, leather shorts and vest.

The House music leaves a ring in those ears.
The funky soundtrack for all those Queers…
'Gym Bunnies' take home their cute "trade…"
Those less beautiful… hope one day to be laid!

The candlelight vigil for those with us no more,
Our tears and memories flow down as before.
The Village Choir laments over their demise.
Pink balloons are then released up to the skies.

Melancholy haunts the Mardi Gras Pride…
The grim reaper wants to take you outside.
A year from now, another face will be gone
Let us just hope, you're not the chosen one!

So party all you L.G.B.T.Q. and curious friend
Hope the music and love will never ever end.
We are God's chosen people, to bring much joy
Seek out the homophobes 'go forth and annoy!'

Beware The Bisexual

He was tall but not too tall, average but not small.
He could be a Justin or a Conrad or just simply Paul.
His jeans went in and out in all the tight, right places
The hair, the cut, the profile, he had one of those faces.

He leant on the bar in just the right way
Not like a drunken fool and not effeminately gay.
He lip synched Kylie, Madonna; all the right tunes.
My eyes where all over him as he made me swoon.

His 'buns' were tight and pert and oh so high…
That front package I could imagine make you cry!
The obligatory white t-shirt left nothing to chance.
Two perfect pecs, a six pack at just one glance.

Several brandies later, I decided to make my way,
I rehearsed my line "excuse me fella are you gay?"
But disaster, a travesty, as he smiled and replied.
"No mate, don't do labels, bisexual" I nearly cried.

So he claims to be bisexual and swings both ways.
One minute charming the ladies, then next the gays.
My life flashed before me, as I imagined the depressing scene,
A long and frustrating sex life, with a gorgeous closet Queen!

The Polychromatic Generation

A Lesbian activist once said to me,
"No more 'going underground' to be free."
At night though we become what we want to be
… and escape the world of heterosexuality.

****

Back in the day, it was sufficient to say, "You're Gay!"
But not with the modern young people today.
Social media neologism, implies the future's bleak…
So they relabel themselves in which to seek…
… more congruence with the skin they are in.
True identity; via the scalpel or reps, at the gym.
No longer is it fashionable, to be who you are.
Everyone craves celebrity and be a little star!
Shun the day light and shine bright at night.
Under the sequinned rainbow, stand and fight!
Bespoke closets, the sexual metaphoric womb…
… as we step out from the shadows and gloom…
To a different time where the law permits,
Gay marriage and divorced lesbians, stick tape to their tits.
Transsexuals now transgender…… on the N.H.S.
The religious bigots claim it's an unnatural mess.
Sapiosexuals love the mind but not… physical sex,
They are not interested, in six packs and pecs.
Heteroflexibility are straights who might oblige,
Six cans of lager they put their inhibitions aside.
Bisexuals, pansexual or just plain confused,
Get any of the new 'labels' wrong, no one's amused!
No more are we 'puffs,' 'faggots', 'dykes' and 'ginger beer.'
All so very confusing, that I'm becoming… a mute queer.
Natural, non-binary and gender fluid, are but a few…
To have become a collection of constants… well, who knew!
The L.G.B.T.Q collective… that we seem to be today…
Could take up to twenty minutes…just to say, 'one's gay.'

Cushion Boyfriend

My boyfriend's a cushion, I hold every night
My boyfriend's is made of fabric, I hold so very tight
My lover is so unique, especially to me
He has no mouth to speak and no eyes, to see

I embrace him as I go to bed, we do not talk
He never leaves my side for he cannot walk
My cushion lover and... I are all that there is
Everything I own is mine and of course... is his

At night I hold him tightly, always from behind
The arrangement suits us and he does not mind
Darkness permits my imagination, to take a hold
My nocturnal lover cares not... that I am very old

Lovers from my past... who sadly did not survive
Are now soft furnishings, kept so very much alive
The contours of their body, their padded frame
Is of no matter as I no longer remember their name.

I grind my hips in such a way to allude that I am there
My cushion boyfriend indifferent is blissfully unaware
I try to envision passion of sexual scenes of old
My body hot with sweat, in contrast the cushion is cold

The passage of time has brought us to this
A genuine boyfriend and lover I do so miss
But until that day... I dream it may come to pass
I console myself with my cushion boyfriend's ass!

After All This Time

Forty-five years is quite some time.
To try and find words that rhyme,
To bridge a gap... a parental void,
When a marriage is mutually destroyed.

As a child you had no control.
Just one day you were simply told,
That one's parents where no more,
One remained, the other closed a door.

The consequences of which, no one knew
The long term effects, quite out the blue.
Like those four Swedes you grew to admire
Their wedding vows, also did sadly expire.

The winner takes it all... is not quite true,
Everyone loses, when all falls through.
A child going through puberty has to learn fast.
The future is the present, the past is the past.

Multitask single parenting is no mean feat.
To fill the gap where the family is incomplete,
As a child you have to step up to the plate,
Always be dutiful, tidy and never be late...

A carefree childhood is sacrificed in a divorce.
Best not to blame anyone and feel remorse.
Just take each day and year as they come...
...with an absentee father and working mum.

Time and emotions mellow with the seasons
Who did what and what were their reasons.
Life dictates what adults we come to be...
One phone call is all it takes and hot cup of tea.

Separated parents' love can be quite favourable…
… as dutiful unhappy unions can be undesirable.
Children just need love, to show them how to fly
They too will leave the nest for life's open sky.

So! Is it better to have two parents, rather than one?
'Tis better to have any parents, than simply have none.

You Didn't Leave A Note

I returned home at the usual hour…
My journey was tarnished by a shower.
The office was a corporate drag…
"Miss Conformity" was your usual gag.

All those office boys all dressed in grey.
The question was which of them was GAY.
I had my doubts about one or two…
But didn't care as I always came home to you.

The bus ride was an utter nightmare…
Public transport as you know, I don't care,
The stopping and starting and those tired faces
I'm not at any point interested in these places.

I just want to get back from my nine to five day.
To be warmly embraced by you in the usual way.
Your strong loving arms and smell of eau de cologne
Reassured me I was with you, well and truly home.

Opening the door, shouting "I'm home honey"
But silence greeted me which I thought was 'funny'
I removed my jacket and kicked off my shoes,
Checking the usual places you often snooze.

Kitchen was void of all aromas and cooking smell.
Not in the bathroom, the door was ajar so I could tell.
I started to re check each and every room…
My heart started to pound as I sensed the gloom.

Something was not right with our usual routine,
You were not there to greet me, as you'd always been.
I had left you this morning in our usual way…
You said 'bring back something big bright and gay'

'Something like me?' "No, flowers you daft queen."
In retrospect I hadn't liked the look of any I'd seen.
I sat for some time just watching the clock,
Hoping to hear the lock of the door or even a knock.

Hours ticked by, a million emotions cruised through my mind
It was now beyond a joke, if it was… it was so unkind.
I made a few phone calls to people we both knew
All confirmed they hadn't seen sight nor sound of you.

It was getting dark and my mind alarms were ringing.
My tired eyes holding back the tears had started stinging.
I now realised the Police where my next option to call.
My head was spinning as I sensed the seriousness of it all.

As I fumbled for my phone there was a sharp knock at the door.
I rushed to open it but was horrified by what I saw!
Two sombre looking police officers asked me my name,
And did I know a gentleman by the name of Wayne

Curtly I snapped, "Of course I do, he's my bloody boyfriend."
They offered their condolences but before they could end,
"What are you saying, why are you here?" their reply stunned!
A body was found in the woods, dead from where it hung.

They asked me of motives and reasons or potential rows
I didn't hear a word of it, time and motion had just froze.
They informed me he was now in the morgue lying in peace
My life partner, the man I love, now just referred to as deceased!

The emotional floodgates scrambled for reasons why,
Why did the man I embraced this morning want to die?
No explanation no indication just a lump in my throat
And it would seem there was no suicide note!

Two people died that day, it is fair to say,
One to be haunted by that horrendous way…
The other was robbed by the actions of that rope,
The other lifeless and living without any hope.

A note was written but was never found…
As the life ebbed away it had fallen to the ground.
The wind had caught it and blew it far away
And the rain erased whatever it was meant to say.

To Kiss (part one)

'Is it wise to kiss a frog?'
He may turn it into a snog!
'Is it wise to kiss a horse?'
Just watch out for those teeth of course!
'Is it wise to kiss a cat?'
Some people just love doing that!
'Is it wise to kiss a dog?'
Not if you are blind in a fog!
'Is it wise to kiss a mouse?'
Make sure you are in a little house.
'Is it wise to kiss a fly?'
If you have the energy, then try!
'Is it wise to kiss a giraffe?'
Well that's just silly and plain daft!
'Is it wise to kiss a dove?'
Well of it implies you are in love!
'But if you want to kiss a 'Panda'
Don't hold your breath and just stand there
It will take some time to get them in the mood
As they don't like bad breath or anything rude!

That 'Norwegian' Saturday Night!

The dance floor full, it was a 'jump-in'
Sadly the door staff where a 'thump-in'
Norwegian sailors were in port this night
Seven foot high and in the mood, to fight!

The music I recall was of an ethnic vibe.
Being the DJ, I choose the music… in this dive!
With hindsight, this was to be the pre-show.
Of something much worse… I was not to know!

Seven days later from this notorious night.
This fight would take on a more fatal sight,
From this dance floor, to foreign shores…
A sinister right wing dance of… racial wars!

I recall he spoke to me, with expletive and calm.
He wore a pale blue scarf, his hand on my arm.
He referred to the music as 'this ni**er shit'
From the tone in his voice, I knew he meant it.

On recollection the 'thank you' seemed cold,
For what was about to happen and unfold!
Politely I replied I could change the style,
Staring at me, he shared an emotionless smile.

That fateful summer's day in a foreign land.
Seventy-seven people's death, he had planned.
Eight died in the 'City of the Christmas Tree…'
Then to an island of young people, on a shooting spree!

It was seven days later that I was to learn his name,
Of the man who murdered and caused such pain.
Recalling that fateful notorious night, I felt quite sick,
The man staring back at me was Anders Behring Breivik!

(NB this is a story of a true encounter in July 2011)

Poem To A Friend

I lost a friend today
A friend no more
I woke... I rose
To find her on the floor

I lost a friend today
The perfect little host
We never spoke a single word
She received, no post

A vacuum... a void
Has entered my life
The loss of a companion
My surrogate wife!

The loss of teeth
Her weeping eye
Her saggy belly
It was no time to die

I lost a friend today
A friend no more
My heart is broken
As I hold her little paw.

Stroking A Cat

Stroking a cat with a gammy eye
That is to say
The cat
Not I

Soft and fury
Just like fleece
This cat that belongs
To Myra Hindley's niece!

Off it goes
To where
No one knows
Unperturbed by
Bygone woes.

'More's' the pity...
As we reflect on sadder times
Contemplating other's
... personal crimes.

For we must face the future
With a happier eye...
That is to say the cat
You and I...

David Bowie 47.16

"We heard the news today oh no!" We moaned.
'The queen bitch' was on the phone, to a sad little gnome.
John 'stopped dancing' wanting a 'rock and roll suicide',
'The man who sold the world' and 'star man' just simply cried.

'Let's dance', but there is no one on the floor to rebel with,
'The jean genie' moves sadly across the floor with a spliff
'Ziggy and the spiders' follow the 'black star' to Mars.
The not so 'scary monsters' pack up and leave in cars.

'The pretty young things' hang their heads and say 'it's a pity',
They run with the 'cat people' to the 'suffragette city…'
'Young Americans' seek 'fame' with the 'golden year' queer.
No one will greet those 'heroes', 'all the madmen fear'

'Blue jean' is extra blue, 'tonight without you',
'Under pressure' without Freddie 'don't know what to do'
'China girl' is no longer in 'fashion' the 'boys keep swinging'.
But eleven 'one o sixteen' David just stopped singing.

The sad news is all over the radio and 't.v.c one five'
The message… 'the Thin White Duke is no longer alive'.
David is swimming with the dolphins far far away…
Until that time we are reunited, on that David Bowie day.

'Ashes to ashes' please inform Major Tom.
That little Davey Jones has so sadly gone!

(Dedicated to Sioux)

Too Shy To Dance

A party was set for July twenty-eight.
The invitation stated... don't be late.
Twinkling lights lit up the summer night,
I felt so excited and positive it felt so right.

The birthday host promised friends I'd know.
Intrigued I promised I would certainly go.
It had been some time I'd been out and about,
I would be okay 'no shadow of doubt.'

I agonised for hours on what I should wear.
To make an impression to show I was there.
Black was the outfit, my colour of choice.
It made a statement without using a voice.

I showered and shaved and got prepared,
But an invited guest was to leave me unprepared.
I arrived later than I had initially planned...
My entrance was subtle and not very grand.

In my younger days, I was the 'belle of the ball.'
Now life's knockbacks had left me quite small.
I smiled and gestured to faces that I knew...
But one individual's face came out the blue!

He was a recent addition, a long lost find.
He certainly stood out and one of a kind.
A missing branch from this family tree...
I stared at him but he looked, right through me!

Afro hair, skin-dark and body pert and tight.
I could have looked at him, for the rest of the night.
My heart did stop I was caught off guard.
In this summer night party in the back yard.

He was introduced to me... and said 'Hi'
His eyes sparkled like stars in the sky.
I felt so ugly, inadequate and out of place,
As I bathed in the beauty... that was his face.

His long lost family were certainly blessed.
By this breath taking young interracial guest.
I managed a pathetic woeful... "hello"
But this breath taking boy dealt me a blow.

At parties I had a reputation to dance
But those eyes had dealt me quite a glance.
I retreated to a corner and studied the floor
He'd seen right through me... I'd become a bore!

Too shy to dance... I stood alone
To the party guests I'd become unknown
'Social rigour mortis'... took control,
Isolated and lonely... I'd lost my soul!

The beauty of youth can disempower
Like a neglected grave and fading flower.

Benefit Beauty

Oh here she comes all wig and tits
She has the look of 'classic council glitz!'
Nobody cares where you're going or where you've been,
Always in the wrong place always on the wrong scene.
The smell of 'poppers' mingles with her odour and scent
Your benefit entitlements are oh so quickly spent!
The cheap 'shock frock' from the market that hardly fits,
A strip of medical tape gives her a cleavage but no tits.
The Avon Lady hasn't been kind to her face
Consider the back end of a bus, cased in mace!
As regular as clockwork there's a knock at the door
It's 'tranny shagger' Mr Kahn your 'quarter to four'.
The client, the punter, the trade that pays the bills
Passively, earnestly they pay for their afternoon thrills.
Bondage, humiliation, vanilla fetishism and role play,
Of course it's all just fun, as she's no woman and he's not Gay.
Discreet adult 'play time' to spice up their tedious little lives
No one gets hurt of course, except the ignorant wives.
Time has not been kind to that ageing face,
You no longer look like a member of the human race.
So here we are again, it's the end of the week,
Fridays and Saturdays never seem as bleak.
Amyl nitrate and vodka your poisons of choice,
The beat of the dance music silences your voice.
You strut and prance for all to see and admire
But they have seen it all before and starting to tire.
Like a sequinned clown in six inch heels and 'lippy'
You fall into the arms of anyone and offer some titty.
But rejected you're flung across the bar and hit the floor
The vodka propels you back up to endure yet more,
Tonight is not your night drunkenly you moan
You head through the door to the streets yet again alone.
You are a drama in stilettos, a nightmare in a frock…
Your thong has gone westward now revealing your cock.
Instinctively you get home and crash into your bed…
Where for the next twelve hours you might as well be dead!

Homeless

Homeless, rough sleepers
Wet rain, drunk, weepers.
Cardboard mattress, concrete sheets,
Human beings litter the streets.
Lampshades are lampposts...
No letterbox for these folks!
Camping out... without 'nowt,
Little Jack Russell watching out.
Sleeping bags and blanket...
Protect them from the climate.
The high street is their street
At night with their cold feet
As we awake to 'Alexa's' voice
Think of those with no choice,
Kerbside etiquette is no place to be
There but for the grace of God, is you and me!

Mad Mel

Mad Mel, has been at it again,
Dealing with life from her windowpane.
Trapped in her apartment living all alone,
Lovers now gone to where, unknown.

The Afro, hair shows signs of grey,
Whites of her eyes, keep foes at bay.
She feels isolated in a causation world.
Craving sane company, this lonely girl.

Some days a joint, just will not do…
The frustrations of life just get through.
A hot bath and long needed soak…
Today was full of comedians, one big joke!

From her window she sees the insanity outside.
The sanctity of home, where she can hide.
Those clowns who turn her hair premature grey.
The utter madness she observes every day!

A lady of standards, on a budget so tight…
Hasn't got the money to make it right.
With problems of her own she stands alone,
Against a world, where reason has flown.

Self-conscious, depreciating 'Mad Mel'
Often wondering "does she smell?"
The menopause only she would know.
Transition of life, emotionally 'all over the show!'

She purrs like a cat; then roars like a lion.
One moment at peace, next like a siren.
Fighting her corner, most of her life.
That glare, that stare; acts as a knife.

She avoids the neighbours, the prejudicial kind.
Life is tough enough she needs peace of mind.
No time for their ignorance negativity and hate.
Like Rosa Parks she has enough on her plate.

Erratic behaviour is just unbridled passion.
The kind that makes white folk...ashen.
Zest and enthusiasm, true to her roots.
Not high-rise, nine to fivers, in cheap suits!

How long will she stand; there no one knows!
For 'Mad Mel' time just simply froze.
Alone at her window, staring at the sky.
She lives in a place where dreams come to die.

Rose

Her face had the allure and charm of landfill.
Pale saggy chest resembled that of roadkill.
Self-harm arms like a crossword puzzle...
The kind of mouth, best suited for a muzzle!

She had a profile like that of Mr Punch,
Not the calibre of lady that did lunch!
Too much reality had marred her life.
Her partner wanted a punch bag, not a wife.

Reading and writing was not her sort of thing,
But a skin full of alcohol, would make her sing.
Snorted, inhaled, injected whichever made her sick
Those quickly spent benefits, universally did the 'trick!'

Police and social workers would help and support,
But too conspicuous to shop lift and always caught!
One of life's characters, rough diamonds we all know
The type of people from an afternoon television show!

Self-inflicted tattoos invariably of dubious spelling...
And a complete lack of self-worth left her smelling.
A lifetime of knocking on doors for sugar or tea,
If it wasn't so tragic it could be deemed, quite funny.

Not one of the beautiful people it has to be said
Her personality and wit made up for this instead!
Empathy and tolerance are her means of survival
That toothless grin and smile is quite the eyeful!

Her 'style' is androgynous, DM's and fatigues.
Her favourite tobacco... always smells of weeds.
Incapable of sitting alone by herself at any time.
Off she would go, for adventure... and petty crime!

Rose by name and certainly in nature for sure…
Roses grow and flourish in the best… manure.
Such is the life of this personality… called Rose,
Life would be the more dull, without …I suppose.

Happy Heroin

A nocturne. Night was her time for fun…
She often smelt of piss, she was 'no nun!'
Stock piling on tin foil and skimmed milk.
Lips like cherries and hair unlike silk!
Not the kinda girl for knitting and sowing.
Her needles kept the diamorphine flowing.
Chasing the dragon her pastime of choice
Inhaling the vapour, she loses more than her voice.
For a moment she rides a 'White Horse' called 'Snow.'
A brown skag beast they all seem to know.
She's a dope on this junk but "she don't care!"
Track lines and debt, she is beyond a prayer.
A state of motherhood that is sad to see…
She does not recall what happened to baby.
Selfishly she is the 'happy heroin addict today'
As for tomorrow, well it is very hard to say…
If she scores then it is a day much as before…
…but if not, she will be a victim dead on the floor!

What on Earth

Oh indeed what on Earth…
That humans give little worth,
All they care about is mankind
Leaving the environment well behind.
Their little homes and smaller cars.
Restaurants to eat, drink in bars
Four walls with music to dance away,
Engines with wings for that holiday
The sea is now plastic, nowhere to swim
Extinctions and global warming is very grim
Eat sleep, break wind then repeat!
The carbon footprint from many feet.
When they are born, mother and foetus scream,
Millions globally, the ultimate bad dream.
Yet another hungry mouth demands to feed…
As the planet reacts to this constant need.
The volcano, tsunami and hurricane
All to help alleviate, the human drain!
They shop, they shout, they fight they breed.
They laugh they cry but humans take heed!
The time will come when you are gone…
As 'Mother Nature' will ensure there is none
Of you… who foul this sacred place,
So good riddance to the human race.
God no longer wants wars in 'his' name,
For it is you… who are mostly to blame!
That egocentric arrogance when you hold a gun.
Uniformed or otherwise it's no joke or fun!
For when you are injured or even die…
The Sun, the Moon, the Earth will never cry.
Your vanity, greed, deception and lies…
Well bring 'peace on Earth' due to your demise!

A Sad Day

So the violins bow does draw a woeful tone,
As the cellist creates a lamentable moan.
The drum pounds a melodic solitary beat
You stood no chance... day is lost, admit defeat.

Negativity did remonstrate, of which you fought,
All your plans and preparations...came to naught!
Outnumbered against your demons and foes...
You had no chance of winning, accept the lows!

Wishes were empty and offered no solace...
A day of no value, of immobility and paralysis.
Like a Gothic statue in a forgotten cemetery,
You recall nothing this day... it voids your memory.

Days like today, the sun is cold, birds are mute.
The wind does blow like a morose weeping flute.
A hunched cellist... draws back his long black bow,
To lament a broken heart... as tears start to flow.

In a solitary place you endeavour to find reason
To continue in the bleak and unforgiving season
Friends whisper that tomorrow is but another day
But sadly in the pale grey sky, hope flew away.

The Umbrella Fella

There was a little fella I once knew
Who'd be there for anyone if feeling blue
Not much to look at, skinny legs, big head
Like a quickly drawn sketch, it could be said.

Funny little fella had a very special charm
When weather was bad he'd protect you from harm
An orange umbrella he would place overhead
Keeping you safe from morning noon 'till bed.

In clothes of green, eager to help if he can
An obliging little soul a helpful little man.
Always ready to protect and lend a helping hand
When the rain is heavy and the sun a little bland.

The umbrella fella is never under the weather
'Positivity is positivity' and he never says never!
With a smile on his face and a twinkle in the eye
His soul purpose is to protect you from the sky.

So be kind to those who protect you from above
Show them great kindness and even greater love
You never know when might need an 'umbrella fella.'
A cheery little fella holding a big orange umbrella!

Kimberley

Slate grey pebbles wet and dry.
Platinum clouds in a pale blue sky.
Black head gulls, cry far out at sea.
Old boats float, beside the quay.

A pod of lobster nets on the shore.
Sand blows along the quiet floor.
All is still and in its place...
The wind it makes pale a thin white face.

A silvery nondescript colourless tableau.
The kind of place only the locals would know.
A cat miaows at the closed fish shop.
Two clay pigeons eye... from rooftop.

A bell at the 'Cozy Nook Café' does ring.
To indicate life, the birds take wing.
A lady in yellow coat and woolly hat,
Sits at the window and smiles at the cat.

She embraces her mug of tea as if a friend,
Alone she sits, time goes on it never ends.
Her mind it wonders from this and that...
Then back to the lost, windowsill cat.

Her absent friend she sees no more...
As she vacantly stares out towards the shore.
Her friend made her laugh, she was funny that way,
But she never said she was going away!

Overalled waitress enquires, 'One tea or two?'
Well she thought, 'Victoria would know what to do.'
She'd been a dinner lady, a good friend of mine.
But she's not been in touch it's been some time!

The waitress takes a call from the wall
To the solidarity customer she does ball...
"Kimberley love, Connie your mothers on the phone...
...t'was just wondering when you'll be home?"

Kimberley stands up, she's very tall...
She glances at the clock upon the wall.
Lamenting the loss of the friend she did not meet,
As she glides down the empty harbour street.

A lonely gull cries far out at sea.
We did not see her demise sadly
Before all it went wistfully wrong.
A distance piano plays a familiar song.

(In memory of Victoria Wood)

MacCrawley The Cat

Benny MacCrawley was a cat from Crab Lane…
He would watch the world go by from the windowpane.
A salubrious fellow with fine whiskers and long tail,
He would make the female cats swoon and wail.

To the human eye he was just a grey furred handsome chap,
But to the feline cats eye, he was a dapper 'cat in a hat.'
With a cocked topper and waistcoat of deep red.
A golden fob watch and a monocle, attached to his head.

Such was the style and finesse of this sublime feline.
Mice they said would faint on traps due MacCrawley's divine…
…beauty personified eyes of deep green, whiskers so long,
At midnight, he would lead the cats' chorus with a song.

Benny MacCrawley the cat would strut along on the wall
Everyone would watch and purr and have a complete ball.
He'd recite poetry and perform 'acro'cat'robats' just for fun.
Curious birds had better watch out as he could certainly run!

Benny's reputation was "a cat of all trades a master of all"
The amazing routines he could do with plastic red ball!
Balls of wool and a fluffy feather thing on the end of a stick
Would keep all who watched him entertained, with every trick!

He was quite the connoisseur of chicken and all types of fish
To be perfectly honest he was grateful to anything in his dish.
Water had to be room temperature and of the bottled kind
He always felt rather vulnerable eating with an exposed behind.

His owners adored him… he was quite the apple of their eye,
Both blissfully unaware of a secret that made him high!
For MacCrawley the cat had an addiction, a certain guilt trip,
He was partial to 'nepeta cataria' better known as 'catnip.'

He would be scenting his territory in the usual routine fashion,
But the breeze would catch his nose and evoke a deep passion.
His back leg would take on an Elvis characteristic shake…
Up like a periscope his tail would go fluffy and off he would make.

Like bees to honey, like flies on a cow pat… off he would go.
To a patch in the garden where the 'catnip' would grow
All his swagger and cool sophisticated style, would now differ,
As he landed like a cat obsessed, rolling about like a 'giddy kipper.'

Paws in the air now facing the sky, he'd wriggle and squirm.
Like one big happy fluffy grey adorable lovesick worm.
In a state of pussy cat ecstasy, he would be exhilarated,
As he frolicked about and was simply quite liberated.

Black birds and blue tits, robins and a curious thrush…
Would come to watch this strange spectacle and "catnip rush"
MacCrawley the cat's, prey would come from quite a mile
To view a cat on its back, eyes closed with that frozen smile!

…but then without warning he would spring to his feet!
Birds take to the sky and the rest run down the street.
Fortunately …he was still groggy from his role in the grass
Oblivious to his fleeting audience he lets this moment pass.

With a spring in his step he takes a running leap to the wall,
Still covered in catnip his co-ordination delivers him a fall.
Unperturbed… he lands on all fours amongst the Rose bed
And decides it's probably time to go indoors…to be fed.

Life is a 'mere bagatelle' for this very fine cat…
With perfect manners he wipes his paws upon the mat.
Today the finest salmon is "le poisson de chiox aujourd'hui"
Then to the windowsill to cat nap until half past three.

Such is the life of Benny MacCrawley this real cool cat
At night in his waistcoat with fob watch and cocked hat
Under the moonlight, high up on his Crab Lane wall…
Singing with the cats' chorus and adored by them all.

The Shorbassi Boat

I spent my life building my ship
Only to find it did not fit.
I could not sail there was no sea.
It only rains when it rains on me!

My sails are vintage feeling old.
My body aches…Tis sad to behold.
The crew of my life abandoned ship
Not prepared to set sail on this trip.

Life delivers me to a strip of land,
God has dealt me a cruel hand.
The onus is on me to make the change
To far off lands that seem so strange.

The kosher sky is full of metal birds,
Fear possesses me I have no words.
So I build my boat for pastures new
To hopefully set sail in a sea less blue!

I drift past the land of Pharaohs shrine.
Where the river flows north, in sands of time.
I pay the guards man to look the other way
Sailing from my place of birth and decay.

At night I lament my heavy aching heart
The woeful day, quayside… I did depart.
I comfort my soul with songs from the past
Downcast and outcast, how long will it last.

I trust in the stars my guides in the night.
To ensure my journey delivers me right…
To the arms of a stranger, not like a mother…
The forbidden love… the embrace of another!

My ship is of my own endeavours and creation
To free me from my perilous situation.
The people from the yellow star night sky…
Want the land of my birth, so I say goodbye.

Too strong to fight back I leave in peace,
Hope the fighting will one day cease.
I continue my journey on my "Shorbassi boat"
And hope to God that I stay afloat…..!

Bilal

I have a 'WhatsApp', 'Instagram' friend…
Countless messages we have started to send.
My 'Chinese Apple', I keep an intense eye…
As I eagerly anticipate his passionate reply.

Sadly, he is far away in an Arabic land,
Of sun sea and disappearing sand…
All is not as it seems in his place of dreams
So we plot and plan, departing schemes.

Average in height but outstanding in fight.
He trains his mind and body for flight…
His ripped toned body… is of the classic kind.
To go unnoticed, one would have to be blind!

His eyes are sunken deep brown and bright.
His smile radiates a warmth of such delight.
Text message and translate, our deepest dreams
From our simple hopes, to our wildest extremes!

Born, fourth day of month five… my Taurus of love
We are as compatible… as peace is to a dove!
Chinese year of the Pig… in ninety-five he came alive,
But this little Rabbit cannot wait for him to arrive.

Bilal… is the focus of my thoughts and future,
He texts with passion, he is my private seducer.
The photographs he sends me… arouse my heart
I cannot bear to be without him, "Oh Cupid's dart!"

A son of Allah, this Arabian Prince of mine.
All my worldly goods, I give to you and sign.
To one day wake and find you next to me…
Would be the ultimate in this sense of ecstasy.

But reality is banality… I'm resigned to text chat.
You in your war-torn country, me in my flat…
Our mutual dreams keep us distracted and free
From my loneliness, your frustration, let's hope and see!

What Could Have Been

I decided to delete you from my phone.
I decided I actually prefer to be alone.
The unpredictability of being part of a pair,
My rose tinted glasses just saw despair!

The simple truth is it must be told...
You are young and sadly, I'm too old.
I pine over your image perfect in my hand,
But your physical presence I could not stand.

Your youth, your beauty energy and smile...
Would feed my insecurities self-loathing and vile.
To be honest I choose solitude and imagination
To the harsh reality and inevitable separation!

I know I made you feel good I was eager to please.
My "you appeal" and positivity is like a disease!
I encourage and speak of a future for us both...
But your presence in my life, I just cannot cope!

Too many years I have lived alone with a solitary heart,
Years and years have passed spent in the dark.
Yes, you were a rare golden light in a darken room...
But I have become quite accustom to my self-gloom.

There is a familiarity to this melancholy of mine,
The clock ticks by to measure my inevitable decline.
I cannot dim the optimism of your shining youth,
It pains me to say all this to you but it's the truth.

I am to roam this world it would seem all alone.
So hence, I shall be deleting your number from my phone.
You are the personification of all that's good and true
But your golden light is unsuited to my ageing blue.

Please forgive me, time is yours... you will forget...
...that I was the one... you did not learn to regret!
You will meet many lovers with that beautiful face,
I will recall it always, in my sad and lonely place.

The Jobbernolls

Shadow cast upon the walls
Vixen screams and cat calls
Trees ripple in the breeze
As statues start to freeze
The hedgehog scurry's through
The night sky is an inky blue.
A platinum moon casts the evening light
The crow's craw and take flight
A breeze blows the leaves away,
Clearing the ground for another day.
The clock tower beckons another hour,
A mischief of mice halt and cower
Rapidly they consume a midnight feast
The farmer's barley, oats and yeast
Mr Tibbs is out on the prowl
Giving the game away, with his yowl.
...and so we leave this nocturnal scene
A midnight routine that has always been.
Vacating this place of shadows and dark
As soon the dawn chorus will once again start
...and the day will be full of the 'jobbernolls.'

Jobbernoll's Day

The jobbernolls of feat; 'farting crackers'
Some work hard and some are slackers
Jockum-gage's upon their heads
The 'member's mugs' place, is under beds!

From dawn to dusk they hurry about
They whisper, then gossip but invariably shout
Dressed to the nines, German for 'no'
All very busy, always somewhere to go.

We have 'fat culls' with much 'gingerbread.'
The gaunt graven like the living dead
A 'buttocks and file' do their best
To enrich themselves from the rest.

A 'balderdash bantling' screams for Mother,
But she is making 'balsom' with her brother!
The 'maggot man' hones in on this 'lullaby cheat'
And steals it away by its screaming feet!

The 'jobbernoll's' hustle and bustle all the day.
God looks down… only to look away.
For ignorance is bliss for all that he sees
Impatiently waiting for that evening breeze.

To blow the 'jobbernoll's' back to their beds
To rest their chatty, banal, vacuous heads
…and leave the night to the river folk of dreams
To deliver them nightmares bedlam and screams.

The Owls of Bentley Lane

The Owls lower their heads at Bentley Lane.
As time will never be quite the same.
Seasons will still come and then they'll go…
Only the Owls will know when he'll show.

In those quite times, he will return to see.
To view his former life in the country,
Whistling Jerusalem with a smile on his face
Resuming his routine in the floral place.

He will cast an eye over the vegetable patch,
And make sure the koi carp are up to scratch
Remembering the times in the little green shed…
His first little home… when he had just wed.

No one will know he is actually there…
You may sense a reassuring warmth in the air.
Unknowingly, you go on with your life,
He will be there to shelter you all… from strife.

Only the Owls of Bentley Lane know he is there
He will continue to return to show that he cares.
To witness the Worboys generations come and go
Protecting them and theirs: from any potential foe.

On a Spring day rest assured he will be there
In the Summertime, he will be with you, to share.
Autumn he will be heard through the leaves of gold
Winter will be warm… with the stories he told.

For Owls are wise and will look after you
All you have to do… is listen to their 't'wit t'woo'
So look to the Owls as they can truly see
Send a message, for the Bentley Lane, 'Bunny'.

Finally in that tranquil resting place..
Peace has now come to your face.
As God comes to seek your company
Your family will live on, in your… legacy.

(Dedicated to the memory of Mr 'Bunny' Worboys)

Mayvis

Twenty-third of March, time marches on
You reflect on where the time has gone
Your sweetness itself, how ironic the demise
All who love you, wipe a tear from their eyes.

The little home shed, once green now black…
You will always be present at the chimney stack,
…but from the Orchard you hear a familiar voice,
That man you married, your first love of choice.

The Owls of Bentley Lane are here again
To end your suffering and ease the pain
He leans on the family garden gate
He smiles and beckons don't be late

Hand in hand you leave the koi carp
The angels accompany you with a harp
Up to the church… upon the hill
"Bring Me Sunshine" you always will

Hair set and flowing… by the staff at Mayfair
Your heart is free and you have no care
Grandpa Rabbit and you… are reunited again
Keeping a close eye on all… from Bentley Lane

As you all look from the windowsill
Now far from the snowy "white white chill"
Off to sunbathe in the all-embracing sun
Through a 'secret rose garden' she and Bunny will run.

At night she will be there with a warm embrace
To reassure and wipe away tears from your face
You're a vision in purple your colour of choice,
With love in your heart…a song in your voice.

So when you are low and feeling forlorn
Stand under the Apple tree, upon the lawn
Think of the love… Mayvis and Bunny did share
And when you heart lightens, you know they are there.

(Dedicated to the memory of Mrs Mayvis Worboys)

Sunflower

Think of a sunflower and think of me.
My face in every bouquet, you will see.
The scent of which, I smell so sweet.
My presence within each person that you greet.

I will be with you in each floral bouquet.
A gentle reminder that I am okay…
I am with family members, on the other side.
Who's loss you marked, for whom you cried.

The sadness will be temporary, it will pass.
I know you all loved this Liverpool lass.
My brother, is here to say 'hello',
Keeping an eye on you all, down below.

In the 'Orchid Garden' we see you there,
Eating with great happiness in your usual chair.
Our love, we celebrate with the best champagne,
To each and every one we recall and toast your name.

The spirit I had for life, I now send to you.
Success and love... in everything you do.
Ever present in the 'Eaton Road' flower shop
Like the flowers there, my head will never drop.

So think of me when the sun does shine
Like the 'sunflower' I will be just fine.
Our day will come, when we meet again
In the 'lavender' flower shop of no pain.

The 'Liverbirds' took me to my resting place.
The Mersey, washed the tears from my face.
Lennon and Cilla invite me to dance, in Sandfield Park.
Well I better go...before it gets too dark!

Sunflowers stand proud, face to the sun,
Just think of me, smile and have some fun.

(Dedicated to the memory of Stan & Susan Hughes)

October Boy

October Boy senses death
He can smell pumpkin breath
October Boy sees the leaves a fall
He can be seen at the Halloween Ball
October Boy is all about the scales
He likes to walk in forests and gales
October Boy turns back time, an hour
Jack Frost freezes the Summer flower.
October Boy the Vampire takes to the street
Tis the season to go fourth to trick or treat.
October Boy eats berries from the trees
A time for coughs and a time to sneeze
October Boy sees trees turn to gold,
He embraces fresh, blue skies of cold.
October Boy bids farewell to the Geese…
Autumn brings its own unique peace!
October Boy adorns himself to keep warm,
He loves the season from which he was born.
October Boy is of a melancholic kind
He is happy to leave the Summer behind…

November Boy

The November Boy has a sting in his tail
He is very strong despite looking frail
The November Boy is tall and strong
And he indulges in all that is wrong.

He likes to drink and smoke and lots of sex
Skinny bowed legs and a perky pumped pec's
The finest red wine... is his drink of choice
It is as deep in colour... as deep as his voice!

The November Boy is sex on two legs
He likes to be adored by those who beg...
The November Boy is a naughty porn star
Admirers come flocking from near and far

Men want to be him and women will faint
Commitment is something, that would constraint!
He is the preverbal party animal... of the night
A Gym toned body under clothes so tight.

The November Boy swings his tail from behind
It's long and hard and not difficult to find.
The November Boy is well and truly blessed
He certainly stands out from all of the rest.

When sober he will talk of symbiosis and fashion.
He will talk with great clarity, insight and passion.
Several bottles and hours later by quarter to four
He will have drunk the party dry and hit the floor!

The November Boy will be familiar to STD's
He will be very aware of that dreaded disease.
The November Boy will always be so much fun.
But when the time is right will go see his Mum.

He lives and breathes for the finer things of life
His wit and intelligence as sharp as a knife.
Sex is as important as the wine that he drinks
From hard-core bondage to furtive winks!

The November Boy is of the wine glass… classes,
Straw noses, cigarettes and bubble butt asses.
The November Boy loves role-play and orgies
Vices and indulgence… he makes no apologies!

Everyone should have a Scorpio in their life…
Don't pin them down to be a husband or wife…
They are pure indulgence and of the extreme
The kind you fantasise about in a wet dream!

The December Boys

The December Boys are the end of year.
Month of celebration goodwill and cheer.
December Boys half man half horse up on the hill,
Thoughtful and considerate and say, "I will."

The architects of life they strive for the best.
Full of ideas and energy and seldom they rest.
Enthusiastically getting plans off the ground…
But often get distracted then they can't be found.

December Boys share their birthday with Christ,
Often getting duel birthday cards which isn't nice.
December Boys just turn on the charm and dance
Winning folk over with a smile and a glance.

Unlike the boys from the month gone before
These have money, style and so much more.
Drink Chardonnay, eat Quail eggs and caviar,
These little mountain goats…can sail so far!

December Boys are your 'Boarding School' types.
Social networkers… one of life's bright lights,
Cricket and Rugby… master of all they survey
So open-minded they have friends that are Gay!

These are your "google boys" a general know all.
Taking photographs of orchids while designing a hall
A true Renaissance lot… a delight to have a round
Quite the eclectic type… that can ever be found.

December Boys have fathers called Bunny,
Their mothers are cute and oh so funny.
The December Boys are never lost in a crowd
Popular and charismatic but never crass or loud.

The December Boys make great friends for life,
Loyal in the good times and of course the strife.
The December Boys are the light, at the end of year...
Lift up your Champagne flutes and wish them good cheer.

Christmas… "déjà vu"

And so it comes to pass, December at last.
The month of twelve, the month so fast…
Where money and cards are quickly gone
A time of mistletoe and kisses cheaply won.

A time of indoor trees, tinsel, crackers and balls,
The chicken and the turkey no longer call.
Crackers go snap, the jokes invariably crap,
Those paper crowns just rip and flap.

The turkey is tasteless and now it's three
No one seems to notice the Queen on TV
The gags are like the homeless, sad and poor,
Constant cheap wine makes us all roar.

Pretend we are having a jolly old time
The whole thing's a lark, a seasonal crime!
Empty boxes, gift wrap thrown… adorn the floor.
As we spend more money like the year before.

Ebenezer Scrooge a true hero of mine…
He knew that Christmas was a great waste of time.
Children indulged in avarice and greed,
As parents forget what children really need.

Gone are the snowy white days of the past
Where no one knows how to really fast.
Bloated egos and stomachs so fat,
The tinsel, the decorations, tacky old tat!

The carols sung by choirs, sing out of tune.
Dear God, will it ever… be all over soon?
We sing of a land no one has seen…
Apart from the Salvation Army with tambourine.

So here we are it's that Christmas again…
A bleak tedious time of spiritual pain.
Puppies will be forgotten and left alone
Neglected old folk waiting by the phone.

Oh when will this odious time come to pass
This obnoxious seasonal drain pain in the ass.
Be replaced by a day more genuine and true
Where its simple meaning is just me and you?

A forlorn Geldof sings of African woes.
Where the heat is too intense for the snows
Send them Peaches a fruit now gone
Where the kosher heroine burnt and shone.

From across the lake, Greg can be heard…
'December won't be magic' Bush that's the word.
Noddy has 'Slade' it again and again!
Dear God. December is such a pain!

Happy New Year (Yet Again)

The fireworks explode with their usual power
As the chimes do toll the midnight hour
The drinkers baptise themselves in the Trafalgar Square
While the others simply throw chairs to the air.
Mythological Father Time yields his scythe yet again
Reaping away the former year, for much of the same
The same faces in the same places…
'Sing Auld Lang Syne' with strange embraces.
The twelve month mantra, out with old in with the new,
Seems rather familiar, melancholic and blue.
Big Ben bells have rung for years
The tedium of the revellers, vacuous cheers.
Bills will always arrive on time; the police thrive on our crime,
Commuters will sit down at nine, then again at six to dine.
The aliens will probably never come, buses, inevitably run.
For some it'll be fun, for others the lottery will never be won.
The house, the gate, the family car…
It's starting to feel like Betjeman's 'Leamington's Spa'.
Bedroom to bathroom, kitchen to gate,
Better to be early never to be late.
So! Fireworks explode on the predictable hour,
As the chimes do toll yet another 'Capricorn flower',
Jools will be there to sing 'hip hip hooray'.
For yet again it's 'Hogmanay'!